Liz Dobbs

KEEP CALM AND POT ON

GOOD ADVICE FOR GARDENERS

Quadrille
PUBLISHING

"*The main purpose of a garden is to give its owner the best and highest kind of earthly pleasure.***"**

GERTRUDE JEKYLL
GARDEN DESIGNER, PAINTER
AND AUTHOR (1843–1932)

The word paradise is derived from the Iranian word *pairi-daeza* meaning an enclosed garden. A place cool, lush and with water, often from a well, in contrast to the open countryside which was hot, dusty and dry.

In winter, the 'bones of the garden', that is its structure of paths and beds, is laid bare and it is easier to see what is working and what isn't. It is also good to revisit gardens you like, out of season; you can pick up why they work – for example, whether it is because the paths are generous or the hedges well clipped.

"My good hoe as it bites the ground revenges my wrongs, and I have less lust to bite my enemies. In smoothing the rough hillocks, I smoothe my temper."

RALPH WALDO EMERSON
ESSAYIST AND POET (1803–1882)

The Secret Garden by Frances Hodgson Burnett, published first in instalments in 1910 then as a complete book in 1911, is a classic for children and adults alike, where the garden is a symbol for the healing powers of living things. The garden transforms two sickly, spoilt children into healthy capable companions and an adult comes full circle from creative delight to sorrow and back again. Needless to say the author was a keen gardener.

A garden where you can see the whole plot from the house may feel empty even if it has a lawn and a bit of border. Try the theatre designers' trick and bring out the 'wings' from the sides of the borders to create some distinct spaces you can fill with interesting shrubs.

> " *The best garden should be a personal expression. It shouldn't matter if the owner of a gas station hasn't studied the principles of Gertrude Jekyll.* "

MICHAEL POLLAN
AUTHOR AND JOURNALIST

'An apple a day keeps the doctor away':
even in Medieval times the apple was used
to cure all types of complaint.
In monasteries, fruit orchards provided
food, drink, a place to stroll and a burial
ground for the monks.
Even if you don't have room for an
orchard, most sunny walls or fences have
room for a couple of varieties of apple
trees trained as cordons.

To make a time-consuming garden more relaxing, look at the high-maintenance elements – do they provide a valuable function and if so how could this be done in a different way? Perhaps trellis instead of hedging; fewer but large flower beds; more perennials and fewer annuals; or a simpler lawn shape to make mowing quicker.

"*I have never had so many good ideas day after day as when I worked in the garden.*"

JOHN ERSKINE
EDUCATOR AND AUTHOR (1879–1951)

A quick trick for an easy lawn is to cut and maintain a small area, leaving the rest as a wildflower meadow. You could cut a path through to a feature or a small clearing. Keep the path and clearing cut regularly to 1in (2.5cm). In time you could have other areas that are left to grow to 3–4in (8–10cm) and some parts can be meadow, which needs cutting only twice a year.

A mowing edge is an edging of brick
or paving set just below the lawn
surface, which allows you to mow
right over. This speeds up mowing
and means you need to trim the
edges less frequently.

You can capture the lemon aroma of the crushed leaves of *Melissa officinalis*, lemon balm, in a fresh herbal tea. Culpepper, the 17th-century herbalist, said it 'driveth away all troublesome cares'. The plant was also known as bee balm; medieval beekeepers rubbed down a new hive with the leaves to calm and settle a swarm. Lemon balm is an easy perennial herb to grow in a pot or in a border, but it can spread and seed around, although if it spreads to your lawn, you get a whiff of lemon when you cut the grass!

Five perennial plants that look good
in a pot:
Spring – *Dicentra spectabilis* to see its
heart-shaped flowers
Summer – *Agapanthus* (move
undercover in winter)
Autumn – the variegated sedge *Carex
hachijoensis* 'Evergold'
Winter – hellebores, to appreciate the
flowers at close quarters
All year round – *Euphorbia myrsinites* is
drought-tolerant with evergreen trailing
stems and long-lasting flower bracts
(irritant sap when cut) in spring

" *The man who has planted a garden feels that he has done something for the good of the whole world.* **"**

CHARLES DUDLEY WARNER
WRITER (1829–1900)

To grow your own calming chamomile tea, use flowers of German chamomile *Matricaria recutita*. For a 'seat' where the aroma can be released when sat on or touched, use the non-flowering *Chamaemelum nobile* 'Treneague'. Or lift a few slabs on the patio and replace with cuttings of 'Treneague' so its aroma will be released as you walk across. *C. nobile* is a perennial but it often dies over winter, so just plant a small area that you can replant from cuttings if need be.

Painting wooden seats, trellis or containers all the same colour is a simple way to smarten up a patio or terrace. Use water-based stains as these are quick to brush on, pleasant to apply and will not harm plants.

> ***"Earth heals me better
> than any medicine."***

MONTY DON
GARDEN WRITER AND BROADCASTER

In Beatrix Potter's *The Tale of Peter Rabbit*, Peter overeats but then feeling rather sick 'felt in need of some parsley' to settle his stomach. Medieval monks used parsley to treat the sick and it is now known to not only be good for the digestion but to be full of vitamins and minerals too. Sow little and often in pots so you have a regular supply through the year and start with a fresh packet of seed each year.

Five good places for different types of
garden ornament:
At the end of a path or alleyway – an
upright figure on a plinth
In a border, emerging from a froth of
groundcover – an empty Ali Baba jar
To mark an entrance – a pair of obelisks
As a centrepiece – a sundial or birdbath
or a sculpture that can be viewed
from all sides
In a shrubbery or woodland – a moss-
covered urn or life-size statue of a
grazing animal.

> **"** *By the time a man reaches forty he is either a drunkard or a gardener.* **"**

FRENCH SAYING

Sharp blades are more effective and less tiring to use than blunt ones. Tools you can sharpen at home using the relevant sharpening stone file include: spades, hoes, knives, scythes and loppers. A local hardware shop might offer a sharpening service or replacement blades for shears or secateurs.

" *All my hurts my garden spade can heal.* **"**

RALPH WALDO EMERSON

ESSAYIST AND POET (1803–1882)

Containers, particularly those made of timber, painted metal or glazed ceramic will last longer if emptied of compost and stored under cover in winter. When stacking pots, store them with the drainage material, e.g. crocks, inside to speed up planting in spring.

Gardening can have a positive effect on the physical and mental health, well-being and social skills of vulnerable adults as it gives them increased access to nature and 'growing things' and the peace of the outdoor environment. Researcher Dr Jo Aldridge says 'They found that taking part in gardening and

related activities actually helped them in other ways. Being outside in the fresh air, undertaking the physical exercise that gardening demands, working with nature and nurturing plants, all helped to improve clients' health and well-being.' (Research by Loughborough University and Thrive.)

"*My garden does not whet the appetite; it satisfies it. It does not provoke thirst through heedless indulgence, but slakes it by proffering its natural remedy. Amid pleasures such as these have I grown old.*"

EPICURUS
PHILOSOPHER (341–270 B.C.)

For somewhere pleasant and relaxing to sit, install an arbour in a sunny yet private part of the garden and train fragrant climbers such as roses or honeysuckle over it.

Cheap trellis is often badly made and flimsy, so if you are on a budget, make your own. A handy tip is to use roofing battens as they are the right thickness for making trellis to fit between upright supports. To make curved tops, use a jigsaw to cut out sections from sheets of exterior-grade plywood.
Use galvanised nails or brass screws for outdoor woodwork.

"*Not every soil can bear all things.*"

VIRGIL
POET (70–19 B.C.)

Birdsong is a delight in the garden.
As well as choosing a bird house
or box to suit particular birds, where
you site it will influence whether
it is occupied or not. Site it away
from direct sun, somewhere sheltered.
Secure well, above ground.
Clean out the bird house at the end
of the season.

Gardening can improve the mental and physical wellbeing of ex-service personnel if it is organised so they meet like-minded people in a relaxed environment. The transition from military to civilian life is eased by being outside and having something constructive to do. Research by Gardening Leave, a charity that offers horticultural therapy to ex-service personnel shows that in order for healing to begin, a person must be relaxed; walled gardens where they are surrounded on all four sides helps them feel safe.

> *"Come quickly — as soon as*
> *These blossoms open,*
> *They fall.*
> *This world exists*
> *As a sheen of dew on flowers."*

IZUMI SHIKIBU
POET (970–1030)

Growing houseplants such as the humble spider plant (*Chlorophytum comosum*) can purify the air in your home or office. NASA scientist Dr. B.C. Wolverton published his research on using plants to cure sick building syndrome in *How to Grow Fresh Air: 50 Houseplants that Purify your Home or Office*. Plants ranged from common foliage specimens such as palms, rubber plants and *Ficus* to potted flowers such as gerbera and azalea.

Look for aluminium shafts on long-handled tools if you find conventional tools heavy and tiring to use.

"*One year's seeding
is seven years' weeding.***"**

ENGLISH PROVERB

To mark out a circle in the garden, for a circular lawn or a bed, all you need is a skipping rope or similar string, a sharp stick and a broom handle. Take a length of rope the same length as the diameter of the circle. Tied the ends together and insert a stout broom handle firmly into the ground. Loop one end of the string over and the other end over a sharp stick. Holding the string taut all the time, mark out the circle.

A simple trick to make your garden feel designed is to give your lawn a defined shape: a simple outline such as a circle, square or rectangle works best. Mark out the area using a garden line then use a half-moon cutter to cut the turf.

"*Sweet flowers are slow and weeds make haste.***"**

WILLIAM SHAKESPEARE
POET AND PLAYWRIGHT (1564–1616)

The *Hortus conclusus* was a Medieval enclosed garden where the lady of a noble house would be able to wander and reflect in safety. A safe outdoor space where we can think and meditate in peace still has appeal; a modern example is to be found as part of Ian Hamilton Finlay's Little Sparta Trust Garden, designed within the walls of an old barn.

The humble garden shed has long provided an area of personal space to hide away – the word is derived from *scead* an Anglo-Saxon word for shade. A roll call of creative shed dwellers includes: Rudyard Kipling, Benjamin Britten, Cicely Mary Barker (author of the *Flower Fairy* books), Roald Dahl, Dylan Thomas and Virginia Woolf. Not forgetting inventor Trevor Bayliss who invented the wind-up radio in his garden shed.

" *All gardening is landscape-painting.* **"**

ALEXANDER POPE
POET (1688–1784)

A wet, heavy clay soil makes planting
bulbs in autumn hard work; instead,
plant dry bulbs in individual pots.
Overwinter them in a cold frame lined
with gravel, then in spring plant them
in the border where you see gaps.

> **"** *More and more I am coming to the conclusion that rain is a far more important consideration to gardens than sun, and that one of the lesser advantages that a gardener gains in life is his thorough enjoyment of a rainy day!* **"**

MARGARET WATERFIELD
GARDEN WRITER AND ARTIST

A **LAVENDER** list

Laundry such as sheets and pillowcases sprayed with lavender water and ironed promotes calm sleep

Aromatherapy: a touch of the essential oil on the temples takes away headaches

Violet flower spikes are a summer feature for every garden

English lavender (*Lavendula angustifolia*) is the most fragrant and garden worthy

Nectar-rich flowers are visited by bees and the resulting lavender honey is much prized

Delicious in small amounts if a few buds are added to shortbread or chocolate

Evergreen and will remain neat if plants are pruned regularly when young

Repels insects if hung up in bunches in the kitchen

Get to know the microclimate in your garden and note which parts are in sun and shade at different times over the course of a year. If there is a prevailing wind, what direction does it come from? Are there beds that dry out in summer or are there puddles on the lawn overwinter? This will help you select the best place for future features and put the right plant in the right place.

❝ *Take thy plastic spade,
It is thy pencil; take thy
seeds, thy plants, They are
thy colours.* **❞**

WILLIAM MASON
POET AND GARDENER (1724–1797),
THE ENGLISH GARDEN (1782)

In a small garden, rather than just opting for little plants choose plants that provide a long season of interest, for example, spring blossom and autumn colour, or a perennial such as heuchera with long-lasting colourful foliage plus flowers.

**❝*Give me Valium ...*
or give me a garden.❞**

ANNE NELSON
WRITER

"God Almighty first planted a Garden; and, indeed, it is the purest of human pleasures; it is the greatest refreshment to the spirits of man."

FRANCIS BACON
PHILOSOPHER, STATESMAN,
SCIENTIST AND AUTHOR (1561–1626),
OF GARDENS (1625)

The 15th-century Italian Renaissance's secret garden or *giardino segreto* was a private garden within the main garden. Inspired by the cloisters of Medieval monasteries, it offered a secret place for reading, writing or quiet conversation.

*"Flower in the crannied wall,
I pluck you out of the crannies,
I hold you here, root and all,
in my hand,
Little flower — but if I could
understand
What you are, root and all,
and all in all,
I should know what God
and man is."*

ALFRED, LORD TENNYSON
POET (1809–1892)

Some early garden design advice from
Leon Battista Alberti (1404–1472)
that still holds today: 'You should place
porticos for giving shade, planters where
vines can climb, placed on marble
columns; vases and amusing statues,
provided they are not obscene.
You should also have rare plants …
Trees should be aligned and arranged
evenly, each tree aligned with its
neighbours.'

Good flowering perennials for clay borders include: *Crocosmia*, hellebores, daylilies (*Hemerocallis*) and peonies. These can be left to grow into clumps year after year.

Three gorgeous shrubs that
thrive in clay are:
Chaenomeles (flowering quince) –
trained as a wall shrub it reliably
produces spring flowers
Cornus (dogwoods) – many different
types, from ones for winter stems to
those with lovely flower bracts
Roses – most do well in clay soils
if given regular toppings of organic
matter.

The sap of a cut leaf of aloe vera (*Aloe barbadensis*) will soothe and heal scalds and burns; grow this succulent as a potted plant on the kitchen windowsill.

" Perennials are the ones that grow like weeds, biennials are the ones that die this year instead of next, and hardy annuals are the ones that never come up at all. "

KATHARINE WHITEHORN
JOURNALIST AND AUTHOR

Plantings in large gardens often lack impact despite many expensive visits to garden centres. Opt for broad sweeps of perennial groundcover under shrubs to cover bare soil and prevent weeds.

To keep costs down, try wholesale nurseries or learn to propagate groundcover plants: hostas and hardy geraniums are easy ones to start with.

"*I have often thought that if heaven had given me choice of my position and calling, it should have been on a rich spot of earth, well watered, and near a good market for the productions of the garden. No occupation is so delightful to me as the culture of the earth, and no culture comparable to that of the garden.***"**

THOMAS JEFFERSON
3RD PRESIDENT OF THE USA (1743–1826)

> *"Plant your own garden
> and decorate your own soul,
> instead of waiting for someone
> to bring you flowers."*

JORGE LUIS BORGES
WRITER AND POET (1899–1986),
TRANSLATED BY VERONICA A. SHOFFSTALL

5 healthy fruits for small spaces: strawberries, blackcurrants, rhubarb, blueberries and dwarf apple.

Formal hedging and features such as box edging and knot gardens need regular trimming. There are now lightweight power hedgetrimmers with extensions and adjustable cutting heads that can make light work of this (though you will still need to collect up and dispose of the cuttings).

" *Your garden may be clipped, neo-classical, random cottage style, modern high-tech, or some intensely personal vision of Byzantium that nobody, anywhere, has ever thought of before. Do not let anyone tread upon these dreams.* **"**

ANNA PAVORD
GARDEN WRITER AND AUTHOR

Borage (*Borago officinalis*) has a taste of cucumber in its young leaves and star-shaped blue or white flowers covered in silver hairs. They were added to wine to cure melancholy in the time of Pliny. Today the flowers are added to summer cocktails where they turn pink.

"In answer to the amateur gardener's eternally repeated question 'When should I?' and 'What's the best time to? I've concluded that nine times out of ten the answer is 'When you're thinking about it; when you're in the mood'."

CHRISTOPHER LLOYD

GARDENER AND WRITER (1921–2006),
THE WELL-TEMPERED GARDEN (1970)

Poor sandy soils are free-draining so as well as being dry they can be low in nutrients too. Six of the best drought-tolerant plants for a sunny spot: *Cistus* (rock rose), *Eryngium* (sea holly), *Kniphofia* (red hot poker), *Perovskia* (Russian sage), *Phlomis fruticosa* and *Sedum* (ice plant).

A hot sunny site in sandy or chalky soil is just the place for a Mediterranean herb garden. Sweet bay, rosemary, sage, thyme, fennel and lavender will all thrive here and as well as fresh leaves for cooking the herb flowers will be visited by insects such as bees.

> **"*What a delight it is*
> *When, of a morning,*
> *I get up and go out*
> *To find in full bloom a flower*
> *That yesterday was not there.*"**

TACHIBANA AKEMI
POET (1812–1868)

Pot marigolds (*Calendula officinalis*) are easy to grow from seed either in herb beds or in containers. Often called 'poor man's saffron' the orange petals can be added to colour cheese or rice. Extracts from the petals are widely used in creams and lotions, as they soothe dry skins.

Displays of containers full of bedding plants can look impressive but they will need daily watering, weekly feeding, regular deadheading and pest control. An automatic irrigation system will help with the watering especially for hard-to-reach hanging baskets but you still need to check it is working as the tubes can become blocked or damaged.

> **"** *What continues to atonish me about a garden is that you can walk past it in a hurry, see something wrong, stop to set it right, and emerge an hour or two later breathless, contented, and wondering what on earth happened.* **"**

DOROTHY GILMAN
NOVELIST

Lemon verbena (*Aloysia triphylla*) has a particularly intense flavour; even a single leaf in hot water makes a refreshing tea. Jekka McVicar, herb expert and nurserywoman, recommends taking the tea last thing at night to ease digestion and for a good night's sleep – it is the only herb she dries to ensure she has a year round supply for this purpose. Lemon verbena is a tender deciduous shrub, tricky to overwinter, so buy a young plant each year.

"What was paradise, but a garden full of vegetables and herbs and pleasure? Nothing there but delights."

WILLIAM LAWSON
ENGLISH AGRICULTURALIST
AND PIONEER CO-OPERATOR (1836–1916)

"*To be overcome by the fragrance of flowers is a delectable form of defeat.***"**

BEVERLEY NICHOLS
AUTHOR, PLAYWRIGHT, JOURNALIST
AND COMPOSER (1898–1983)

Lawns are often seen as a chore as they need regular mowing and the clippings collected. Or do they? Matching the power of the mower to the size of the lawn and looking for handy features such as easily adjustable cutting heights and easy-to-remove grass collectors can make a big difference. There are now mowers with a 'mulching option' that can cut the clippings very fine and then disperse them back onto the lawn to feed the grass. Also could the lawn size be reduced or the shape simplified to make mowing quicker?

Gardening has been identified as
one of the activities associated with
wellbeing and enhanced physical health,
particularly with regard to community
garden projects. Most studies express
the benefits of natural landscapes
or green spaces in terms of stress
avoidance or alleviation. Other psycho-
physiological benefits recorded have
included: improved cognitive function;

improved self-discipline; alleviation of attention-deficit disorder symptoms in children; reduced incidence of illness or reported illness; pain relief; improved relaxation; and coping with trauma – as well as unusual indirect effects of stress reduction such as reduced crime. (*RHS Gardening Matters: Urban gardens 2011* brings together international research on how gardens affect urban areas)

> **"** *There is material enough in a single flower for the ornament of a score of cathedrals.* **"**

JOHN RUSKIN
WRITER AND ARTIST (1819–1900)

Crush the leaves of mint as you wander around the garden and the aroma instantly refreshes you. Many cultures use mint in recipes, from the strong peppermints for teas to the spearmints used in cooking.
Mint is invasive in the garden, so grow each type in its own pot and keep it moist.

There is no need to spend hours staking border plants such as delphiniums so their top heavy flower stems are supported – there are now hundreds of alternative herbaceous perennials that add height but are self-supporting, including ornamental grasses. Positioning plants with more space between them also leads to stronger stems as overcrowded plants tend to stretch up to the light.

❝*There is no gardening without humility. Nature is constantly sending even its oldest scholars to the bottom of the class for some egregious blunder.***❞**

ALFRED AUSTIN
POET (1835–1913)

Dill (*Anethum graveolens*) has a warm aroma, and its feathery foliage and seeds aid digestion. It is an annual plant that quickly runs to seed.

" *How fair is a garden amid the trials and passions of existence.* **"**

BENJAMIN DISRAELI
BRITISH PRIME MINISTER
AND AUTHOR (1804–1881)

A dark dingy pathway can be 'greened' with shade-loving plants such as pot-grown hostas, cyclamen, ferns and climbers trained on trellis to create a jungle trail.

*"More than anything,
I must have flowers,
always, always."*

CLAUDE MONET
PAINTER (1840–1926)

> **"***You raise flowers for a year; you see them for but ten days.***"**

CHINESE PROVERB

Fennel (*Foeniculum vulgare*) is a tall feathery herb, either green or a lovely bronze, topped with yellow flowers. Its aniseed flavour was valued by ancient Egyptians, Greeks and Romans as it aids digestion. The seeds were often chewed on fasting days. It is worth growing today as a foliage plant and as a herb for fish, but it can self-seed around.

> **"***I am not a greedy person
> except about flowers and
> plants, and then I am afraid
> I become fanatically greedy.***"**

MAY SARTON
POET AND NOVELIST (1912–1995)

A pointing trowel (for pointing
brickwork) makes a precise yet
lightweight weeding tool
in small spaces such as raised
beds and rockeries.

Clean mud and plant sap off tools before putting away. Carbon steel heads need to be wiped with an oily rag to prevent rust. Hang up hand tools on hooks in a shed or garage. Close the blades of cutting tools before putting away or use a scabbard or holster. Bamboo canes can be sorted into same lengths and stored in a length of drainpipe.

" *The hardest thing to raise in my garden is my knees.* "

ANONYMOUS

To fill in gaps in a perennial border, use bedding plants with daisy-type flowers and a natural habit such as marguerites or felicias.

To fill in gaps between shrubs in a border, use vigorous trailing bedding plants to weave in between them as this is easier than planting lots of small compact plants. Good ones include Surfinia petunias, *Bidens ferulifolia*, *Verbena* 'Silver Anne' or *Scaevola aemula*.

> **"**_What though his phlox and hollyhocks ere half a month demised?_
> _What though his ampelopsis clambered not as advertised?_
> _Though every seed was guaranteed and every standard true –_
> _Forget, forgive they did not live!_
> _Believe, and buy anew!_**"**

RUDYARD KIPLING
POET AND WRITER (1865–1936)

Garlic (*Allium sativum*) has been eaten for thousands of years and a diluted garlic solution will kill bacteria, fungi and even viruses. The health benefits are well known but less well known is how easy it is to grow even in small spaces. Simply plant cloves in well-drained soil in a sunny spot on the shortest day and then harvest on the longest day.

"*Gardening is not a rational act.*"

MARGARET ATWOOD
NOVELIST AND POET

With plants such as tomatoes and courgettes that need a lot of daily watering, it is easy to water in a rush, too vigorously, which washes away the soil from the roots. Insert a small empty plastic plant pot (with holes) nearby at the time of planting, then water into this which will act as a reservoir.

Acid-loving shrubs that make great container plants include: Japanese maple, *Camellia japonica*, smaller rhododendrons such as *Rhododendron yakushimanum* types, blueberries and *Skimmia japonica*. Use an acidic (ericaceous) potting mix and water with stored rain water when possible.

"*In order to live off a garden, you practically have to live in it.***"**

FRANK MCKINNEY HUBBARD

CARTOONIST AND HUMOURIST
(1868–1930)

Rosemary (*Rosmarinus officinalis*) is a hardy evergreen shrub that will grow well in a sunny spot in well-drained soil; just a few of its needle-like leaves will add pungent flavour to foods. If you are short of space grow a prostrate one in a pot. Any trimmings added to a charcoal barbecue or fire produce a lovely aroma.

Ten plants worth buying
as large specimens:
Japanese maples, *Arbutus unedo*,
Amelanchier, bamboo
(clump-forming), camellia,
Hamamelis, holly, magnolia,
Pieris japonica and wisteria.

> **❝***To forget how to dig the earth and tend to the soil is to forget ourselves.***❞**

MAHATMA (MOHANDAS KARAMCHAND) GANDHI
POLITICAL ACTIVIST, LEADER
AND FATHER OF THE INDIAN NATION
(1869–1948)

The botanical name of sage, *Salvia officinalis*, is derived from the Latin *salvere* meaning to be in good health: sage aids digestion and is an antioxidant. In the garden, use the sages with pretty coloured foliage such as 'Tricolour' and 'Icterina' and keep taking cuttings so you can use young plants in mixed containers and baskets.

If you find it difficult to water summer flower containers daily, try drought-tolerant plants such as diascias, gazanias, geraniums and zinnias. Many Mediterranean herbs are also drought-tolerant. All these need sun.

"I'd rather have roses on my table than diamonds on my neck."

EMMA GOLDMAN
POLITICAL ACTIVIST AND WRITER
(1869–1940)

A threadbare lawn can be rejuvenated by sowing grass seed either on bare patches, or by sowing over the whole area if the entire lawn is thin but still has 50 percent grass. The best time of year to do this is spring or early autumn. Birds will eat the grass seed so you will need to net the area until the seed has germinated.

To tackle a lawn with long grass.
First, walk the route to check for hidden
objects. Then cut down grass with a
power trimmer. Let it recover then use
a rotary mower on its highest setting.
After the grass has recovered the height
can be gradually reduced.

Angelica (*Angelica archangelica*) was known as the angel herb for its healing powers. It is an imposing biennial in moist ground whose flowers are a magnet for beneficial insects. When made into essential oil, it makes a relaxing bathwater.

> *" He who shares the joy in what he's grown spreads joy abroad and doubles all his own. "*

ANONYMOUS

Runner beans (also known as pole beans) can be grown against a sunny wall or up a wigwam of bamboo canes – they are very prolific and if you pick the right variety the flowers look good too. The red-and-white flowered 'St George' is one of the best performers.

“*All gardeners know better than other gardeners.*”

CHINESE PROVERB

Annual climbers will grow fast to cover plant supports; they only last one year so will not weigh down their supports and there is no pruning to worry about. They do need a sunny site and care to keep them growing steadily without a check.

Three of the best are:

Sweet peas (*Lathyrus odoratus*)
for scent and colour

Black-eyed Susan (*Thunbergia alata*) with orange, yellow or white flowers; this only reaches 3ft (1m) so it's good in a container

Climbing nasturtium (*Tropaeolum majus*)
which does well in dry, poor soils

A collection of scented-leaved pelargoniums grown in terracotta pots on a sunny patio or up steps will lift your spirits when you gently bruise their leaves. Many can also be used in cooking or cosmetics. There are hundreds of varieties with scents ranging from 'Attar of Roses' to citrus aromas, spicy tones or apple. They are not hardy so you either need a greenhouse to overwinter them or to buy a collection anew each summer.

Most people's spirits rise to see roses in a garden. They offer beautiful flowers, fragrance and some even have colourful rosehips. But choose your variety with care – rather than buy one for its pretty name, look for those with reliable disease resistance and check the expected height and spreads. Careful attention to watering, feeding and pruning can help roses resist disease.

> ## "*I am the fonder of my garden for the trouble it gives me.*"

REGINALD FARRER
NATURALIST, EXPLORER AND
PLANT FINDER (1880–1920)

A common mistake is to buy an item such as an ornament, container or table that is too small for the setting. To get the scale right, mock it up in the garden using bamboo canes and tape, view from all angles and note the dimensions that work. Always take a tape measure with you when shopping for the garden.

"There is nothing pleasanter than spading when the ground is soft and damp."

JOHN STEINBECK
NOVELIST (1902–1968)

Snowdrops (*Galanthus nivalis*) are brave little bulbs that flower in very early spring, and so are a welcome sign that winter is on the way out. Grow *en masse* under trees if you have the room, or in small pots. Rather than buy dry bulbs, it is best to buy and plant them 'in the green': that is, after the flowers are gone but while the leaves are still present.

Quick scents for a patio:
Heliotropium (cherry pie), *Hesperis matronalis* (sweet rocket), *Lobularia maritima* (sweet alyssum) and
Nicotiana alata or *N. sylvestris* (tobacco plant).

A hammock slung between two trees or a hanging chair under a tree is the perfect place for a spot of restorative reading or snoozing.

Be sure to get the right balance between 'active' and 'passive' relaxation in your garden: digging, planting, weeding and pruning are all good exercise but also take time to sit back and look at what you have achieved.

"A garden is not made in a year; indeed it is never made in the sense of finality. It grows, and with the labour of love should go on growing."

FREDERIC EDEN
GARDENER AND AUTHOR (1828–1916),
A GARDEN IN VENICE (1903)

Bare soil between plants will quickly fill up with weeds and stress neighbouring plants. Either you need to weed regularly or add a mulch such as a 2in- (5cm-) deep layer of bark chips to retain moisture in the soil by reducing evaporation and suppress weeds.

10 easy vegetables to grow for
healthy living:
beetroot, beans, courgette, kale,
garlic, leek, salad leaves, potatoes,
spinach (or Swiss chard) and
tomatoes.

"*The garden that is finished is dead.*"

H. E. BATES
AUTHOR (1905–1974)

Al fresco entertaining checklist: clean and tidy the surfaces guests will use, set up pleasant and comfortable seating, freshen up (by deadheading) and arrange bold groups of container plants.

Even a small garden can have a water feature which brings senses such as sound and touch into play as well as sight. A water feature set into the wall of a courtyard can soothe, blocking out the noise beyond. Pumps with fountain attachments can make ponds that gurgle, bubble or even create a mist, whereas a still water pool will reflect its surroundings. Effects should be gentle, so research the right-size pump for the feature and take time to adjust the flow and sound so it is just right.

"*Green fingers are the extension of a verdant heart.***"**

RUSSELL PAGE
LANDSCAPE ARCHITECT (1906–1985)

"Gardening offers a considerable amount of freedom, the refining influences of poetry and beauty, contact with intelligent, interesting people, and health and happiness to mind and body."

VISCOUNTESS FRANCES WOLSELEY
GARDENER AND AUTHOR (1872–1936),
GARDENING FOR WOMEN (1908)

Bog garden beauties; these flowering plants
will pretty up the edge of your pond:
Astilbe – summer flower spires in a range of
colours
Caltha palustris (marsh marigold) – spring
flowering buttercups
Iris laevigata – lavender blue flowers in
summer
Primula japonica (Candelabra primulas) –
elegant flowers in lots of colours

Improve a clay soil by putting a
mulch of well-rotted organic matter
on top that will gradually work its
way into the clay. This will open up
some air spaces and help prevent
waterlogging over winter. If you need
to dig, wait until the soil has started
to dry out in the spring.

There is no one best colour for healing or calmness: so much depends on personal preference and cultural attitudes. So please yourself which colour you choose but a restricted palette will be more soothing than a little bit of everything making a jumble of colours.

"If we persist, I do not doubt that by age 96 or so we will all have gardens we are pleased with, more or less."

HENRY MITCHELL
GARDENING WRITER (1923–1993)

On a warm summer evening, white flowers appear cool, tranquil and almost luminous, so include some in your planting. However, remember that an all-white garden on a wet dull day will look, it has to be said, dull!

Find out whether you soil is acidic or alkaline by using a simple inexpensive test kit that will measure the pH. Most garden soils will be between pH5.5 and pH7.5, neutral soil is pH7. A slightly acid soil (pH6.5) is ideal for lawns, fruits and many shrubs.

A soil with a pH greater than 7 is alkaline: plants such as roses, hydrangeas and fruiting plants such as raspberries may look sickly with yellowing foliage; instead grow clematis, thymes, vines or wildflowers.

"Let no one think that real gardening is a bucolic and meditative occupation. It is an insatiable passion, like everything else to which a man gives his heart."

KAREL ČAPEK

WRITER AND AUTHOR (1890–1938),
THE GARDENER'S YEAR (1931)

A sloping garden can be hard work and a grass bank steeper than 1 in 3 is difficult to mow safely. If it is sunny you might be able to convert it to a wildflower meadow and just cut it once a year with a trimmer.

Terracing a slope is expensive but will give your more flat spaces for seating and for flower beds with the spaces linked by steps.

Children love being in a garden. Use your plot to build happy childhood memories for your young visitors: teach them to make daisy chains, get snapdragons to open their 'mouths', use buttercups under the chin to check who likes butter. Children make good strawberry and pea pickers.

Planting daffodils in autumn is an easy way to be sure of spring cheer. Most are fully hardy and cope well with growing in grass, wet ground over winter and, unlike many bulbs, will take a bit of shade. For containers, look for dwarf daffodils as their foliage will not be so noticeable after the flowers have gone.

❝Working in the garden gives me something beyond the enjoyment of senses. It gives me a profound feeling of inner peace.❞

RUTH STOUT
GARDENING WRITER (1884–1980)

A hot sunny garden needs somewhere cool for relaxation and somewhere to sit in the shade – perhaps you have a large tree you can put a seat under? If not, a climber-clad pergola could cover either a walkway or a seating area. A pond, rill, fountain or waterfall can provide a cool oasis in the sunniest part of the garden.

> **"***The best place to seek God is in a garden. You can dig for him there.***"**

GEORGE BERNARD SHAW

PLAYWRIGHT AND AUTHOR (1856–1950)

Use spring-flowering bulbs under and between deciduous shrubs; by growing early they make use of the light that reaches them before the shrubs come into leaf. Only a few plants will cope with dry soil at the foot of a shady wall or hedge: try foxgloves with an underplanting of ferns, honesty (*Lunaria*) and sweet violets (*Viola odorata*).

Sunflowers (*Helianthus annuus*)
bring out the happy child in
everyone. They are easy to grow from
seed in spring and come in lots of
different sizes; apart from the well-
known giant specimens there are
dwarf ones which are perfect in tubs
or as an edging to a veg plot.

Windy gardens need shelter for plants to establish. A windbreak will shelter an area eight time its height. So for most small to medium gardens, a 6–7ft (2m) windbreak is adequate. A living windbreak is the best long-term solution – either a hedge or a mix of trees and shrubs – but make sure the plants you use are hardy in your area. Allow five years for the windbreak to become fully effective; you might need a temporary non-living one in the meantime.

"*One of the most delightful things about a garden is the anticipation it provides.***"**

W.E. JOHNS
WRITER AND PILOT (1893–1968)

> **"** *If only one were as good a gardener in practice as one is in theory, what a garden one would create!* **"**

VITA SACKVILLE-WEST
AUTHOR, POET AND GARDENER
(1892–1962)

If you don't feel up to climbing a tree
why not give it a hug instead? Tree
huggers claim that this engenders a
sense of wellbeing and oneness with
nature; many recommend the spring
equinox or autumn equinox as the
ideal time.

A large or old tree does not necessarily need to be either tolerated or completely removed. A qualified tree surgeon can advise on a whole range of other options from crown thinning (to let more light in to the ground beneath) to crown lifting (removing some of the lower branches). Ask for the cut wood to be chipped and left for you to compost or use around the garden as a mulch.

Watching wildlife in the garden helps you unwind. To attract birds, butterflies and bees add features such as a garden pond, berried shrubs, nectar-rich flowers such as buddleja and let the edges of your lawn grow longer to encourage wildflowers. Avoid using chemical pest controls, aim to garden organically and leave the birds and ladybirds to deal with the greenfly.

"*In the spring, at the end of the day, you should smell like dirt.***"**

MARGARET ATWOOD
NOVELIST AND POET

No other plant is more resistant to wear than grass but if you have an area where grass is growing poorly here are some alternatives:

Mentha pulegium (pennyroyal) – aromatic creeping mint for moist shade

Origanum vulgare (oregano)– aromatic for a warm, free-draining soil

Thymus serpyllum (wild thyme) – drought resistant, aromatic

Clipped box (*Buxus sempervirens*) – balls, squares or spirals add year-round structure to blowsy cottage garden flower beds.

" *The number one problem in gardening is putting a five-dollar plant in a fifty-cent hole.* **"**

RALPH SNODSMITH
GARDENING BROADCASTER
AND AUTHOR (1939–2010)

Cheer up your spring garden with
a display of tulips; no other flower
offers such a range of colours and
forms. But plan ahead and buy
dry bulbs in autumn and plant
generously in pots before winter.
Top the pots with a layer of fine grit
to deter squirrels and to keep the
flowers free of soil splashes.

To stop a clematis making a 'bird's nest' tangle at the top of the plant and flowering where you cannot see the blooms, remember to prune it at planting time. After planting, cut the stem back to the lowest pair of strong buds. This sounds drastic but will encourage it to branch out lower down. All types of clematis benefit from pruning after planting whenever they are planted. The subsequent pruning in future years depends on the type of clematis.

Regal lily (*Lilium regale*) was discovered by plant hunter Ernest Wilson in western China in 1903. With its heavenly summer scent and white trumpet blooms that almost glow in evening light it brings a touch of class and tranquility to evenings on a patio. Plant dry bulbs in plastic pots and either sink them in borders to fill or put bulbs in terracotta pots on a patio or terrace. Watch out for red lily beetle and pick off and destroy them.

Nearly one in three disabled people believe that gardening has ongoing health benefits, while almost one in five report it has helped them through a period of mental or physical ill health. (Research by Thrive – a charity that promotes the benefits of gardening.)

" *Unlike people, gardens never strive for perpetual youth – they want to look old from the day they were born. Their greatest glory comes with maturity.* **"**

THOMAS D CHURCH
LANDSCAPE ARCHITECT (1902–1978)

"_You don't have to garden to garden; gardening in the mind is a gentle vice with an impetus of its own._**"**

MIRABEL OSLER
GARDEN WRITER

To make seating areas more relaxing create a sense of enclosure by bringing the planting out from the wall or boundary. Or erect a pergola, trellis screen, veranda or overhead sail for shade and privacy.

> **"***It took years to learn what would not grow here. I like to say I have the greatest catalogue of plants in my compost heap.***"**

HAROLD EPSTEIN
PLANT COLLECTOR AND WRITER,
(1903–1997)

Growing fruit, vegetables and herbs helps the rehabilitation of stroke survivors especially if they eat the results. Beetroot helps regulate blood pressure, strawberries relieve joint pain and have plenty of vitamin C and parsley is also nutritious.

> **"***Walnuts and pears
> you plant for your heirs.***"**

ENGLISH PROVERB

The steeper the steps the more awkward they are to use. The ideal height of the step riser outside is 4in (10cm) – much lower than indoors. The tread, or step depth, should be in proportion to the riser. Allow a tread of 18in (45cm) for a 4in (10cm) riser. Outside steps that feel a little steep can be redeemed by installing an outdoor handrail on one side.

A wildlife pond can be any size or shape but the sides have to be shallow with at least one side planted to give cover. If you need to top up a wildlife pond in summer when the water level drops, try to use stored water from a water butt rather than tap water which contains chlorine.

When questioned, people who regularly take part in 'green' activities, 90 percent said it was the combination of nature and exercise that had the greatest effect on them. 94 percent said that green activities had benefited their mental health by lifting depression. (Research by mental health charity Mind)

> **"***The gardener has just as many allies as enemies among the fauna of his garden.***"**

HUGH JOHNSON
WRITER AND EDITOR

Clean up without chemicals – a pressure washer will spring-clean paving, furniture and decking, but check the instructions to check softer materials are not damaged by the high-pressure spray.

> **"***You do not need to know anything about a plant to know that it is beautiful.***"**

MONTY DON
GARDEN WRITER AND BROADCASTER

Dr. Roger Ulrich of Texas A&M University conducts research on the effects of healthcare facilities and nature on medical outcomes. He has found, for example, that patients with hospital window garden views have quicker recovery times from surgery than patients viewing a wall.

Where a mature perennial plant has ceased
to flower or just flowers at the edges of
a clump, dig it up in autumn or spring.
Discard any old, diseased or dead material.
Divide up the youngest and healthiest
sections into fist-sized sections containing
both root and shoot. Fork in some soil
improver and replant the sections. Water in
well and they should grow away well and
future flowering will improve.

Taking part in gardening can make
a child feel happy and boost their
development. Children in schools that
encouraged gardening became more
resilient, confident and lived healthier
lives. Easy food crops for children to
grow in pots include: radishes,
loose-leaf salad, strawberries and
potatoes (in sacks). (Research published
by *RHS Gardening in Schools 2010*.)

Gardening can be educational as well as fun. TV gardener and author Alan Titchmarsh recalls when he discovered gardening, 'From the minute my grandfather took me to his allotment I was hooked for life. Watching how plants grew and getting my hands dirty brought fun and learning together.' To help children grow flowers from seed, try: nasturtiums, sunflowers and marigolds.

"Restraint is a fundamental principle of good gardening. Simplicity brings a sense of calm, whereas too many ideas and too much variety creates a sense of restlessness."

PENELOPE HOBHOUSE
GARDEN DESIGNER AND WRITER

Cleaning the algae off white birch stems with a damp cloth will show them at their best in winter; mature plants whose bark is peeling can be hurried along by gentle rubbing to reveal new skin underneath.

> *"Very broadly, the higher each step is, the faster one goes up them — and a garden, however large, isn't a place for rushing about."*

JOHN BROOKES
GARDEN DESIGNER AND AUTHOR

Most pruning is done in late winter
to early spring when the plant is
dormant but members of the Prunus
family need to be dealt with in
early summer to reduce the risk of
silverleaf disease entering via the
pruning cuts.

Charles Darwin created his 'Sand-walk'
or 'thinking path' in his garden at Down
House in 1846. An area of garden was
fenced off and planted out with native
trees and a circular path dressed with
sandy gravel around the edge. Strolling
around this path every day helped Darwin
to think, and he counted the number of
circuits he took with flints piled at the
beginning of the walk. He would measure
the difficulty of any problem he was trying
to work out by the number of stones he
had placed before solving it.

A variegated shrub that throws up an all-green shoot should have that shoot removed as soon as it is seen. If left, the all-green shoots will be more vigorous than the variegated shoots and will eventually take over the plant.

" *The first gathering of salads, radishes and herbs made me feel like a mother about her baby — how could anything so beautiful be mine?* "

ALICE B. TOKLAS
AUTHOR (1877–1967)

One jasmine, *Jasminum officinale*, offers summer scent that really lifts the spirits, described as being both calming and an aphrodisiac! Grown as a climber, it is happy in any sunny aspect but a warm sheltered spot will bring out the fragrance.

Another jasmine, *J. nudiflorum*, brings winter cheer in the form of yellow flowers on the bare stems of a scrambling wall shrub.

Hand pruners or secateurs will
cope with stems that are ½in
(12mm) diameter or less but if
you have to tackle thicker stems,
use a pruning saw.

" *Structure is the most important component in a successful planting; colour is important too but it is a secondary consideration.* **"**

PIET OUDOLF
LANDSCAPE ARCHITECT

Marshmallow (*Althaea officinalis*) has been known since ancient times for its gluey properties (think of the chewy sticky consistency of marshmallow sweets). Young leaves and shoots were eaten, but in addition the cleaned chopped roots were made into an infusion which was put on soft pads and used to soothe tired eyes.

Shrubs with fragrant winter flowers
lift the spirits in the depths of a dark
season, so plant near them a path
so you can make the most of them.
Most established plants can have a few
bare stems cut and brought into the
house where the warmth will open
the flowers and release the fragrance.
Noted examples are Chinese witch hazel
(*Hamamelis mollis*) and wintersweet
(*Chimonanthus praecox*).

"*Bulbs intrigue me the most. I like the way they shoot into flower, do their thing, and then thoughtfully put themselves away again. I positively relish the fact that so often I forget I have planted them. Then at the appropriate season, there they are, not the slightest bit put out that I have not been worrying about them or making them special snacks.*"

ANNA PAVORD
GARDEN WRITER AND AUTHOR

Water butts or other storage containers for water should have lids on to prevent debris falling into them. Even so they should be cleaned once a year, using a garden disinfectant diluted according to the manufacturer's instructions. You could add your pots and trays at the same time so you start the season with clean pots and fresh compost.

"*Life begins the day you start a garden.*"

CHINESE PROVERB

Editorial Director Jane O'Shea
Creative Director Helen Lewis
Editors Lisa Pendreigh, Sarah Mitchell
Designer Claire Peters
Production Director Vincent Smith
Production Controller Aysun Hughes

First published in 2011 by
Quadrille Publishing Limited
Alhambra House
27-31 Charing Cross Road
London WC2H 0LS
www.quadrille.co.uk

Cataloguing in Publication Data: a catalogue record for this book is
available from the British Library.

ISBN 978 184949 096 2

Printed in China